The Moral Foundations of United States Constitutional Democracy

by

James H. Rutherford

DORRANCE PUBLISHING CO., INC.
PITTSBURGH, PENNSYLVANIA 15222

TABLE OF CONTENTS

The Moral Foundations of United States Constitutional Democracy was written for students of Western civilization and teachers of ethics, law, history, and government. It develops a framework for understanding moral and political philosophy. The framework takes into account several different aspects of human nature and the world in which we live. This provides a basis for understanding several different aspects of universal equality, the unifying "central idea" or primary moral concept of our form of government. The several aspects of universal equality are also traced historically as they developed in different ethical and legal systems of Western civilization. Constitutional democracy in the United States attempts to integrate and balance the several aspects of universal equality as they apply to the coercive powers of government.

I
Introduction

At a time when many nations are throwing off the yokes of totalitarianism and dictatorship it is important that we understand and convey properly the moral foundations of United States constitutional democracy. Those moral foundations at the most fundamental level are not based on capitalism, simple majority-rule democracy, or even freedom. The moral foundations of United States constitutional democracy are based on *several* aspects of universal equality as they relate to the coercive powers of government.

Furthermore, to understand past and current political issues in the United States it is necessary to appreciate that our constitutional democracy is a dynamic system. Our Constitution attempts to incorporate in a pluralistic society several ethical considerations as they relate to the coercive powers of government. This is because the primary concept of equality entails several aspects of human nature and the world in which we live. The Constitution attempts to include several substantive and procedural concepts of equality by first limiting the powers of government and then by dividing and balancing those powers which are delegated to government. Only by referring to the government of the United States as a *constitutional* democracy, however, can we understand and convey to others

1

that it is a dynamic system in which the moral foundations are formed by several aspects of universal equality.

One of the reasons we have some difficulty in understanding the moral foundations of our form of government is that the founding documents presumed that there was a consensus on such matters and therefore do not provide much explanation or commentary. The moral principles and goals of our government, for example, are clearly stated in general terms in the Declaration of Independence and the preamble of the Constitution. *Federalist 39* also makes it clear that the Constitution was meant to be compatible with "the fundamental principles of the Revolution" (Hamilton, Madison, and Jay [1787-88] 1961, 240). The Declaration of Independence, however, describes its primary moral assertion that "all men are created equal" to be a self-evident truth. Later in his life, Thomas Jefferson wrote that the aim of writing the Declaration of Independence was "to place before mankind the common sense of the subject" and he described it as "an expression of the American mind" with its authority resting on the "harmonizing sentiments of the day" (Foner 1950, 802).

Garry Wills did much to clarify the contemporary usage and meanings of such phrases in his book *Inventing America: Jefferson's Declaration of Independence*. He also concurred, however, with an earlier Jefferson scholar, Douglas Adair, who wrote:

> An exact knowledge of Jefferson's ideas...is still lacking....We know relatively little about his ideas in the context of the total civilization of which he was a part.... Until all of Jefferson's ideas and projects are carefully examined against the background of contemporary European developments, and until his theories are appraised as part of the great tradition of Western social thought, we will be unable to take the true measure of the man. (Wills 1979, xxv)

Indeed, the moral assertion that "all men are created equal" has several origins in the Western tradition and derives from several sources of authority which provide the foundations of United States moral, legal, and political thought. A second reason we have problems understanding both Jefferson and our moral foundations has to do with the English language. Our language has only one word for equality when, in fact, we mean at least four different things by the use of this term in the moral, legal, and political philosophy of Western civilization. As an analogy, our language has only one word for love, but the classical Greeks distinguished four different meanings of love with four different words, *epithymeia, eros, philia,* and *agape.* We have a similar problem with the word justice which historically has been closely associated with the concept of equality.

This ambiguity has led to a third problem. As George Orwell observed, totalitarian regimes often distort and invert the truth by corrupting the meaning of words and language. For example, totalitarian communist regimes have, at least in theory, advocated equality as the common ownership of the means of production, but have actually denied political equality as well as the moral agency of other people. Unfortunately, a great deal of intellectual energy has been spent on rebuttal, not by clarifying and defining the *several* aspects of equality and the moral foundations of our *political* system, but in attempts to justify capitalism, distributive justice, inequality, and our economic system in an isolated context.

It would be ironic to accept as a premise of public discourse on constitutional democracy the ideology of Marxism which portrays the economic system to be primary to and determinative of the political system, rather than just an integral and interdependent part of society and government. What is important to recognize is that our economic system, for example the extent to which we are a regulated capitalism or a social welfare state, is determined by constitutional and legislative political processes based on equality. Given such political processes based on equality, it is not irrational for a people to recognize defined property rights, reward production and merit, and incorporate several aspects of distributive justice.

A general *framework* for understanding both the composite and integral aspects of human nature and the world in which we live will be presented and used to help clarify the several different meanings of universal equality. As a tool for understanding, this framework also provides a good reflection of how we have historically defined, understood, and institutionalized the several aspects of universal equality which form the primary moral foundations of United States government.

In 1795, Fisher Ames, a congressman from Massachusetts, perhaps recognized the indeterminate but dynamic aspects of our system of government when he compared it to monarchy in the following way. "A monarchy," he said, "is a merchant-man which sails well, but will sometimes strike a rock, and go to the bottom; a republic is a raft which will never sink, but then your feet are always in the water" (Bartlett 1968, 491).

II
Universal Equality as the
Primary Moral Concept

In 1856, before his presidency or the beginning of the Civil War, Abraham Lincoln said:

> Our government rests in public opinion. Whoever can change public opinion, can change the government, practically just so much. Public opinion, or [on?] any subject, always has a "central idea," from which all its minor thoughts radiate. That "central idea" in our political public opinion, at the beginning was, and until recently has continued to be, "the equality of men." (Basler 1953, vol. II, 385; see also Jaffa 1982, chap. XIV)

A few years ago we celebrated the one hundredth anniversary of the Statue of Liberty, and many would consider liberty, or freedom, as the fundamental moral concept on which our government was founded. Freedom, however, has little meaning outside of one's moral concept of justice. Freedom can mean simply license, the absence of any social obligation or moral constraint. Being a free moral agent does not necessarily mean that one will choose to be moral. Freedom does not address the need to maintain order, establish justice, or provide for the general welfare. Nor does freedom provide much protection from the coercive powers of government unless it means "liberty for all" (Basler 1953, vol. IV, 168-69). Indeed, what we often desire is freedom from the arbitrary will of others.

Morality, on the other hand, provides a context of responsibility for freedom. Morality even implies a degree of freedom of choice and, to the extent of that freedom, responsibility. Freedom by itself implies a type of existential or subjective responsibility but not necessarily any other type of moral acknowledgment. When Jefferson put forth the ideals of our country in the Declaration of Independence, his first assertion, his primary self-evident truth, was that "all men are created equal." The unalienable rights of life, liberty, and the pursuit of happiness were thus put within an ethical context of equality and reciprocity. Jefferson and Lincoln both understood universal equality to be the primary moral concept of American constitutional democracy.

Others have also understood universal equality to be the primary moral concept. Marvin Meyers in his book on James Madison, *The Mind of the Founder,* concluded that, "in Madison's view of man," equality was the fundamental term (1981, xxii). Alexis de Tocqueville, in *Democracy in America* (1835-1840), "advanced the influential thesis that equality is the fundamental theme and characteristic of American civilization" (Davis 1990, 11). Tocqueville noted that even tyrants value freedom, but only for themselves. He also understood that equality is not an extrinsic leveling term but conveys an inherent mutual respect which also implies an equality of political freedom. David Brion Davis, a prominent historian of the institution of slavery, has even concluded that the real antithesis of slavery is not freedom but equality (Davis 1990, 29).

G. K. Chesterton wrote, however, that the belief in human equality is not "some crude fairy tale about all men being equally tall or equally tricky" (see McWilliams 1979, 184). It is not like a Procrustean bed of Greek mythology into which all persons are forced to fit by stretching them on a rack or cutting off their legs. For Jefferson, universal equality was instead a moral assertion — an assertion that affirmed both his own humanity and his own individuality against tyranny. Using fable and analogy, in the manner of George Orwell, one could say that if you are a mallard and don't like ducks or duckhood, then there is going to be an inherent problem with your own self-affirmation by definition. This is one sense in which Jefferson's assertion that "all men are created equal" could be considered a self-evident truth. It is an affirmation of our own humanity.

It is this recognition of his own humanity, however, that allowed Jefferson to also assert his own individuality, not by a will to power and coercion, but by inverting that to a resistance to the tyranny of others. By recognizing the moral agency of others, as well as asserting our own mature responsible personality, there opens up the possibility of deciding political issues by the deliberation of democratic constitutional and legislative processes, rather than by simple coercion, domination, or privilege.

The future of American government still rests on public opinion. It rests on our understanding and support for the moral foundations of constitutional democracy and our ability to communicate and preserve such an understanding effectively. This is important, for the enjoyment of individual freedom and the progress of human liberty are not inevitable. They are contingent, to a large degree, on our willingness and ability as moral agents to place our free will within ethical constraints. It is indeed the self-imposed ethical or moral foundations of government that change mere obedience to the coercive powers of government into a sense of consensual responsibility for a moral duty, a just order, the common good, or human rights. In United States constitutional democracy these ethical concepts all relate historically to the "central idea" of universal equality.

A Brief Historical Survey of Four Different Aspects of Universal Equality Which Make It an Accommodating or Unifying Moral Concept

Universal equality has several different aspects. It can be arrived at as an ethical concept, an affirmation of our humanity and a moral vision of the world in which we live, from several different directions. This is because there are several different aspects of human nature and several different perspectives of the world in which we live. It is the several aspects of universal equality, however, that make it an accommodating or unifying moral foundation of government in a pluralistic society.

Before developing an analytical framework for moral and political philosophy, it will be helpful, as a point of reference, to look at four different aspects of universal equality in the historical context of four different ethical and legal systems. Within Western civilization there developed several sources of moral authority for law and several corresponding ethical and legal systems. Canon Law, Roman Law, English common law, and the social contract theory associated with constitutional law each had a different primary source of moral authority. Each of these systems of law was, consequently, based on a different type of ethical system, and each focused primarily on a different facet of human nature. Constitutional democracy integrates aspects of these four ethical and legal systems as they relate to universal equality and the coercive powers of government.

Canon Law, for example, was based on the authority of God and related primarily to what it understood to be the soul of man. Its ethic is deontological, *deon* meaning "duty" in Greek. That is, it is based on a universal duty "to love God with all thy heart, and with all thy soul, and with all thy strength, and with all thy mind; and they neighbor as thyself" (Lev 19:18, Deut 6:5, Lk 10:27, Mk 12:29-31). Canon Law contains universal ethical principles based on a reverence for God and reciprocity towards one's fellow man. The equal dignity and worth of all persons in this religious system derives from a belief that God not only created humanity, but that man and woman were also made in God's image (Gen 1:27). Equality is intrinsic and not derived from one's individual attributes, but from the relationship between God and humanity.

Roman Law, on the other hand, incorporated significant aspects of natural law based on the authority of a perceived natural moral order in the universe. Such a natural moral order could be understood by all persons, it was believed, because all humans share a capacity for right reason, an ability to know right from wrong. All of the various people within the vast Roman empire, for example, could be expected to learn and know that it is wrong to steal. The ethical system of natural law is primarily normative (based on norms or ideals). Universal equality in classical civilization is based on all human beings having a capacity for right reason and also on a concept of reversibility which requires a rational imagination and empathy.

Aristotle, in his *Poetics,* described reversibility as one of two major elements in Greek tragedies. The second element is catharsis, part of which is a realization that we all, even heroes and kings, have character flaws and are also subject to fate, both of which can lead to a reversal of fortunes. An ethic based on reversibility is not just archaic. In the first century, Rabbi Hillel taught, "What is hateful to thyself do not do to another. This is the whole Law, the rest is commentary" (Shab. 31a). It is also the basis, however, of the Kantian categorical imperative that one cannot place oneself outside of morality without implicitly permitting others to do the same. Reversibility was also a primary moral reason in the thought of both Jefferson and Lincoln in their opposition to slavery (Basler 1953, vol. II, 532; Jefferson [1785] 1972, 163). The more recent concept of John Rawls in *A Theory of Justice* (1971) of justice as fairness, with an original position in which one does not know either his or her fate or circumstances in life's game, is an extension of the concept of reversibility.

Common law in English feudal society derived its moral authority from yet another source — not from God or nature, but from social custom and tradition. This was primarily a communitarian ethical system. It related to the social conscience of the people based on their ethical concepts of rights and responsibilities in society. Traditional English rights progressively became a basis of communal solidarity.

Finally, the social contract theory associated with constitutional law derives its moral authority beginning with the individual in a state of nature concerned primarily about his own safety and happiness. Its very premise is not only that all are free and equal in a state of nature but that everyone is also endowed with natural rights which they are entitled to defend. Such a theory is based on individual concerns and contract. The universality of social contract theory as it applies to democratic processes and constitutional law, however, makes it essentially a humanitarian ethic. It contains an ethic of universal equality based on what we now refer to as human rights and a just claim to resist the violation of those rights.

American constitutional democracy integrates and balances these four ethical systems as they apply to the several aspects of universal equality and the coercive powers of government. The accommodating common moral concept is not just a deontological ethic, with concepts of reverence and reciprocity, relating to God and a person's soul; nor is it just a normative ethic, based on concepts of right reason and reversibility, relating to a perceived moral order in nature and our capacity to understand that order with our reason; nor is it just a communitarian ethic, with concepts of social rights and responsibilities, as they relate to the several aspects of society and our social conscience; nor is it only a humanitarian ethic, with a concept of human rights and the right to resist tyranny, relating to our individual lives and our fundamental needs and desires. The accommodating or unifying moral concept is universal equality which can be derived analytically, and has been derived historically, from each of these sources of authority and aspects of human nature.

III
An Analytical Framework
for Moral and Political Philosophy

A general analytical framework for moral and political philosophy, which incorporates four aspects of human nature and
relates them as cognitive modes to four aspects of the world
in which we live, can now be developed with this brief historical context in mind. Evolutionary theory, for example, postu-
lates such a developmental interaction between an organism
and its environment. Evolutionary theory aside, however, an
interaction between human nature and the world in which we
live is also a very practical matter. In *Jurisprudence: Principles
and Applications,* for example, Ervin H. Pollack distinguishes
between philosophy in theory and philosophy in practice.
Concerning the latter he states that "The criteria from which
we study the world and its relationships are derived from the
world itself" (1979, xiv).

For the purpose of general analysis, four aspects of human
nature or roughly four capacities or cognitive modes at which
our minds function, will be considered. These are appetite
(which relates to our primal needs and desires), social conscience, reason, and interpretation. The premise is that our
moral thought is not unlike the development of our other
mental behavior. It begins, like the cognitive development of

the child, with concrete thinking, and progresses to social concepts, logical reasoning and finally abstract concepts of meaning and purpose which also serve an integrating and narrative function. (This is in part a modification on the work of Lawrence Kohlberg in *The Philosophy of Moral Development: Moral Stages and the Idea of Justice* [1981], which itself is based on the work of Jean Piaget.)

In Western civilization, these four aspects of human nature or cognitive modes have been loosely associated with our need to deal with several aspects or perspectives of the world in which we live. The four mental capacities or cognitive modes are loosely associated with our own individual primal needs and desires, with society, with the natural world in which we live, and with metaphysical or religious questions. The premise here is that our mental capacities develop in response to a corresponding and widening field of experience or perception of reality concerning the world in which we live. For example, our appetite relates to our individual primal needs and desires, our conscience to our social relationships, our logical reasoning relates primarily to the natural world in which we live, and our capacity for interpretation relates to our need to deal with metaphysical or religious questions.

One is tempted to relate this progressive cognitive development also to a model of the evolution of brain structure described by Paul MacLean as the *triune brain* (Sagan 1977, 57-83; Konner 1983, 147-152). The triune brain is a model for the progressive evolutionary development of three layers of the forebrain which MacLean believes can still be distinguished neuroanatomically and functionally in our own brain structure. He describes first a "reptilian complex" which surrounds the midbrain and which probably evolved several hundred million years ago. It relates to such primal instincts as sex and aggression. This is surrounded by a limbic system which is fully developed in mammals but not in reptiles. This he relates to emotions and a social capacity other than primal hierarchy. Surrounding the rest of the brain is the neocortex, which in humans makes up about eighty-five percent of the brain and is associated with reason. To this model one could easily add, at least functionally, the language centers in the left hemisphere of the brain and the capacity for abstract thinking which includes interpretation as integration and narrative.[1] Also, the concept of the evolution and development of capacities rather than anatomical levels is more appropriate, for the brain is a very dynamic structure and highly integrated from top to bottom.

Without obscure anatomical detail and from introspection alone, however, we are aware that we tend to integrate our accumulated thoughts, feelings, and actions into a sense of identity or self and interpretive narrative concepts of orientation and meaning. It is also apparent that we interact with other people and our environment, though never with complete certainty and sometimes not even very well. On the one hand, it is easily demonstrated that our minds affect our perception of reality. Two people, for example, may see the very same thing quite differently. On the other hand, St. Thomas Aquinas and others have felt that the mind also conforms to reality. For the purpose of *general* analysis, the framework I am proposing loosely relates four capacities or modes of cognition of our composite and integral nature to four different aspects of the world in which we live. It is the extreme complexity of human nature, our relations to the world, and the course of history that make such categories useful as a *framework* for understanding.[2]

The general analytical framework I am proposing and will apply to our concepts of universal equality and constitutional democracy can also be seen, in this context, to be derived from the work of Leslie Stevenson, a Lecturer in Logic at the University of St. Andrews. It is a modification of the method of analysis he uses in *Seven Theories of Human Nature* (1987). He maintains that the best way to understand the ideas of any political philosophy or philosopher is to consider the underlying assumptions concerning the nature of the universe, the nature of society, and the nature of man. Since the Copernican revolution, however, Western civilization has tended to separate questions concerning the nature of the universe into those of science, relating to the natural world in which we live, and those of metaphysics and religion, relating to our broader interpretation of identity, orientation, and meaning.[3] The analytical framework proposed here, therefore, would consider assumptions related to four rather than three aspects of the world in which we live, to include metaphysical as well as scientific concepts of the universe. Corresponding to this, the analytical framework also considers four modes of cognition to include the interpretive, integrative, and narrative aspect of thought (which relates to metaphysics), as well as the more immediate, logical processing and calculating component of reasoning (which relates more to science and the natural world in which we live).

For the purpose of general analysis, again, the framework I am proposing relates four capacities or modes of cognition of our composite and integral nature (appetite, conscience, reason, and interpretation) to four aspects of the world in which we live (our own individual primal needs and desires, society, nature, and metaphysical aspects of the universe). This analytical framework is important for its reflects on how we have defined, understood, and institutionalized the *several* moral aspects of universal equality.

It is understood that our categories of thought are significantly influenced by our culture and language. It is also understood that, from an anthropological standpoint, most societies have been based on tradition and kinship-descent lines and without formal written laws. Still other societies have been what Max Weber (1864-1920) described as charismatic in the source of their legitimation and organization (Weber [1921] 1964, 328). From an anthropological viewpoint, what Weber calls legally-based societies have been relatively few. Pluralistic societies based on law are almost an exception. Yet, it is in legal systems and the language of law that our own particular historical ethical traditions and theories have been brought to action or limitation of action concerning the coercive powers of government.

IV
The Several Aspects of Universal Equality as They Relate to the Moral Authority of Law, the Coercive Powers of Government, Integration, and Constitutional Democracy

The Moral Authority of Constitutional Democracy is Based on Both "Higher Law" Concepts of Equality and Democratic Procedural Concepts of Equality

The moral authority and legitimacy of law, corresponding with this analytical framework, can be based on metaphysics or religion, on nature, on some aspect of society, or on the individual. In Western civilization we have developed "higher law" concepts of authority based primarily on Judaic and Christian monotheism and the concept of natural law which was developed in classical civilization. These "higher law" sources of moral authority are not dependent on either our social or our individual will. The following description of natural law was derived primarily from Stoic philosophy by Cicero:

> There is in fact a true law — namely, right reason — which is in accordance with nature, applies to all men, and is unchangeable and eternal. By its commands this law summons man to the performance of their duties, by its prohibitions it restrains them from doing wrong. Its commands and prohibitions always influence good men but are without effect upon the bad. To invalidate this law by human legislation is never morally right, nor is it permissible ever to restrict its operation, and to annul it wholly is impossible. Neither the senate nor the people can absolve us from our obligation to obey this law, and it requires no Sextus Aelius to expound and interpret it. It will not lay down one rule at Rome and another at Athens, nor will it be one rule to-day and another to-morrow. But there will be one law, eternal and unchangeable, binding at all times upon all peoples; and there will be, as it were, one common master and ruler of men, namely God, who is the author of this law, its interpreter, and its sponsor. The man who will not obey it will abandon his better self, and, in denying the true nature of man, will thereby suffer the severest of penalties though he has escaped all the other consequences which men call punishments. (Sabine and Thorson 1973, 161-2)

The concepts of universal equality in "higher law" tend to be intrinsic and qualitative such as the dignity and worth of the individual.

Western civilization also developed concepts of law in which society and the individual serve as the source of moral authority and legitimacy. Examples of these would be the socially-based communitarian common law of English feudal society and its reinterpretation as social contract theory based on the free and equal individual in a state of nature. Rights and responsibilities in feudal societies were based on status and tradition, but they were also of a contractual nature. Universal equality in contractual concepts of law tends to be quantitative and numerical, as in a utilitarian ethic, or as in government by consent with one person, one vote, which is the basis of the democratic process. These are basically procedural concepts of equality.

Constitutional democracy combines qualitative, substantive, "higher law" concepts of justice and universal equality derived primarily from classical civilization and Judeo-Christian religion with quantitative, procedural concepts of justice and equality derived primarily from the communitarian ethic of common law, republican traditions, and social contract theory. Thus, universal equality is both the fundamental qualitative moral principle of our system of government and the basis of the fundamental quantitative democratic process by which it was ordained and ratified, and by which it functions. These different aspects of universal equality were partially reconciled by a democratic constitutional process in which the sovereign people verified a commitment to certain qualitative or substantive "higher law" concepts of equality as they relate to the coercive powers of government. Furthermore, they required a super-majority for any subsequent amendment of these principles in our constitutional law.

The fundamental law of the land, except for the possibility of another constitutional convention, is placed beyond the reach of a simple majority. That is, two-thirds of the Congress and three-fourths of the states are required to amend the principles in the Constitution. To this extent, however, even the choice of those principles to be included in American constitutional law rests on public opinion.[4]

Government as Coercive Power and Its Limitation and Regulation by the Constitution as a Social Contract Based on Equality

What distinguishes moral philosophy as it applies to political philosophy is that government is communal and it concerns primarily the use of coercive power. Taxation is essentially a coercive power. In addition, one of the purposes of government is to ensure social order and thus remove individuals from an escalating cycle of personal revenge. Government, in one view, can be considered a monopoly of coercive power (Weber [1921] 1964, 154). The problem then becomes not only the moral authority of government, but also the limitation and regulation of its coercive power.

One of the strengths of what historian Adrienne Koch called the *great collaboration* between Jefferson and Madison was that between them they had a balanced appreciation of both the possibilities and the limitations of human nature and our capacity for self-government (Koch 1964). The political philosophy which underlies the founding documents thus reflects a concern for both the moral foundations of government and for the limitation and regulation of governmental power. The Constitution, which incorporates this political philosophy, was perceived to be a social contract, a fundamental law of the land which was ordained and ratified by the people. The concept of government as a social contract, however, has not always led to the limitation and regulation of governmental power.

Writing at the time of the Puritan Revolution and civil war, Thomas Hobbes (1588-1679) had argued in *Leviathan* (1651) that sovereignty is not based on divine right or even a *summum bonum*, a highest good, but on the ability and power to establish order. Whatever "Mortall God" could impose order on man's natural state of "warre of every man against every man" had and deserved the implied sovereignty of the people. This "Mortall God" could also define justice and law where previously there had been none. In the state of nature, as perceived by Hobbes, all persons are equal in that they fear a violent death and they are all not only capable of killing one another but are also free to do so. With such a pessimistic view of human nature, Hobbes had the state establish order (chap. 13). In contrast, Jean Jacques Rousseau (1712-1778), writing at a time prior to the French Revolution, had an ambiguous but optimistic view of humanity in a state of nature. Theories based on his writings would later attempt to have the state also define morality, not by simple imposition but by associating it with the concept of the general will. Revolutionary movements in continental Europe — from aspects of the French Revolution to the Russian Revolution, from Communism to Fascism — were based on such unlimited concepts of all order and morality being defined by the state.

John Locke (1632-1704) had a more moderate concept of humanity in the state of nature, and therefore a more moderate concept of the social contract and the role of government. He considered individual rights to precede the formation of government. He reasoned from that premise that society could place limits on the coercive powers of government or even change the government by revolution for good cause. The concept of a social contract as the authority for government served Locke's purposes well. By placing all sovereignty in the people, rather then relying on a constitutional tradition of mixed government that included the king, Locke was able to provide a rational foundation for government by consent, parliamentary supremacy, and the Glorious Revolution of 1688.

Thomas Paine, in *Common Sense* (1776), also used the concept of the social contract. He felt that the mutual benefits and concerns of society in a state of nature preceded government. He also recognized government as a coercive power, however, and he wrote that "Government, even in its best state, is a necessary evil, in its worst state, an intolerable one" (Paine [1776] 1982, 65). Before Paine, the thirteen colonies had focused their grievances mainly on England's Parliament. The Parliament had both violated traditional principles of constitutional law and denied the colonies representation which stood for the concept of self-government. In addition, Paine attacked the king, the whole concept of monarchy, and thus solidarity with England. Locke's arguments for legitimate revolution and popular sovereignty were now brought to bear against the whole government of England, both the Parliament and the king. Paine argued for declaring independence and called for a "Continental Conference" to form a "Charter of the United Colonies." "But where, say some, is the King of America?", he wrote, and he answered, "...that so far as we approve of monarchy, that in America THE LAW IS KING" (Paine [1776] 1982, 96-98). American government was to be constitutional, or in the words of Chief Justice John Marshall in *Marbury v. Madison* (1803), "a government of laws, and not of men." Government was to represent the people not just in theory; it was to be accountable to a fundamental law of the land ordained and ratified by the people and to a democratic process.

The American development of constitutional democracy formally combined the earlier medieval English concept of government as limited by law and the concept of government by consent. Our Constitution was originally perceived to have moral authority both because it contained "higher law" concepts of freedom, equality, and justice *and* because it was ordained and ratified by the people (Corwin 1955, 4). Because the sovereignty of the people was formally expressed in a written constitution and the Supreme Court was given a power of judicial review, neither parliamentary supremacy nor monarchy established themselves in the United States. Through a constitutional process certain principles and values were placed even beyond the reach of transient legislative majorities. It is our Constitution that both limits and divides governmental power and gives it political accountability on the basis of several aspects of equality.[5]

Moderation and Integration by Balancing the Several Different Aspects of Universal Equality

United States constitutional democracy begins with some of the same premises as the classical Greek philosophers, and yet it reaches somewhat different conclusions. Similar to the philosophy of Aristotle, for example, it does assume that man is a political animal, meaning that people naturally desire to live in a *polis*, or community. However, unlike Aristotle, who divided the world into Greeks and barbarians, our form of government gives more recognition to the universal aspects of the human community. Indeed, it was not Aristotle, but his pupil, Alexander the Great, who developed the concept of *homonoia*, meaning concord, as a practical matter of developing unity within his diverse and pluralistic empire. It was also during this period of Hellenism that the Stoics developed more fully the concept of a moral law of nature which all persons could understand by their shared capacity for right reason. The Stoics also superseded the perspective of the Greek city-state with the concept of the *cosmopolitan*, meaning citizen of the universe.

Also similar to the classical Greek political philosophers, our form of government recognizes both the composite nature of human beings and the need for moderation. The teaching of Socrates had been to "know yourself." Plato in his description of justice taught that you should also be true to yourself, especially as to what is your particular merit and what you deserve or is your due. Aristotle was the philosopher of temperance, moderation, and the "golden mean." Of course, if you really know yourself, and are really truthful or honest with yourself and about what you deserve, then it becomes obvious why we should all act with some moderation.

Each of these classical Greek philosophers, however, to a greater or lesser degree attempted to achieve such harmony and moderation in the individual and in society on the basis of reason, which they considered the highest function of human beings (Nagel 1972).[6] United States constitutional democracy attempts instead to achieve accommodation and moderation in a pluralistic society first by limiting the powers of government and then by applying a system of checks and balances to the different functions of government, rather than creating a hierarchy based on intelligence, religion, class, power, tradition, or paternalism. Universal equality achieves some moderation when the concept of the dignity and worth of the individual is understood as a matter which requires the consideration and balancing of at least four different capacities and perspectives. It is important to recognize, however, that this moderation by balancing, which constitutional democracy attempts to achieve, does not portray or understand such ethical questions as *What is obligatory?*, *What is good?*, *What is fitting?*, or *What is humane?* to be based only on material considerations of utility, simply arbitrary, totally relative, or merely subjective. This differs from situational ethics in that all the considerations remain grounded in the concept of universal equality and concern primarily the coercive powers of government.

Within this analytical framework, it is understandable that there are particular consequential ethical considerations as well as more abstract, universal metaphysical obligations and values. On the other hand, it is understandable that particular facts, or what we believe to be facts, are not the sole determinants of values. Moral obligations are not always the same as the positive laws of the state. Natural rights or human rights are not the same as just unfettered individualism. Yet, there remain valid natural, social, individual, and even transcendental claims if a person affirms their self and their humanity, the premise of community, and a concept of continuity.

In this framework of analysis, integration is concerned internally with a reconciliation of our mind's four capacities of interpretation, reason, conscience, and appetite. External integration relates to a reconciliation of our metaphysical ideas, our relation to the world in which we live, our relation to society, and our own individual self-interest. This is perhaps better understood by examining the opposite concept of alienation. Discord and alienation often result when one of our levels of understanding is emphasized to the exclusion of the others, or when, as a society, we develop ideologies that relate to one of our concepts of metaphysics, nature, society, or human beings, but to the exclusion of the other three. In a pluralistic society, there is a potential political problem when only one aspect of human nature is emphasized or when any aspect of human nature is excluded or not taken into consideration. The importance of the concept of alienation in Western civilization can be seen in two of its major systems of belief. Monotheism considers sin to be alienation from God and one's fellow human beings. Marxism considers the problem of capitalism to be man's alienation from himself.

The Institutionalization of the Several Concepts of Universal Equality in United States Constitutional Democracy

In attempting to achieve integration or accommodation on the basis of equality, our system of government does leave the question of meaning and purpose to the individual. This is what Jefferson, following Aristotle, meant by the "pursuit of happiness," which is quite different from the pursuit of pleasure as we understand it. The level of function that interprets, integrates, and narrates meaning, purpose, and continuity in our lives, and deals with the ultimate questions of metaphysics and religion, is separated from the coercive powers and structure of government. Historically, this developed first in Western civilization as both conflict and the sharing of powers between church and state, then as a doctrine of religious toleration in England, and finally as both the disestablishment of religion and the freedom of religion from the coercive powers of government in the United States of America.

Individual conscience is protected and it remains, of course, reflected in our culture, our public opinion, and in our government policies. The individual moral personality is, in fact, the basis of both our constitutional principles and democratic processes. The free and equal individual with moral responsibility is the basis of communal solidarity. The stated general purposes of our Constitution can thus be both to form a more perfect union *and* to secure the blessings of liberty to ourselves and our posterity.

The powers that are delegated to government are divided into executive, judicial, and legislative functions, which are then integrated by checks and balances rather than by placing them in a hierarchy of order. The separation of powers is a fundamental part of the Constitution. The different functions of these divisions of government to make, adjudicate, and enforce the law are somewhat analogous to the specific stated purposes of government in the Constitution to promote the general welfare, establish justice, and maintain security and domestic tranquility. Each division of government, therefore, has a different function and a different primary moral concern as well as a duty to uphold the entire Constitution. Each is also institutionally accountable to constitutional principles and democratic processes based on equality.

The different divisions and functions of our government remain to some extent connected historically to ethical and legal structures which relate to our capacities of reason, conscience, and appetite and our need to deal with nature (unity and order), society (social justice), and our own individual interests (general welfare). The older organic metaphor of the body politic can still be recognized. We still, for example, refer to the chief executive as the "head" of state. The divisions of government in classical and medieval mixed governments were by social class. The divisions of government in United States constitutional democracy are by function and they are accountable to principles and processes based on equality. In addition, however, none of the functions and moral purposes of our divisions of government are by themselves determinate. It can easily be argued that the accommodating concepts of constitutional democracy are the basis of American pragmatism. Our government recognizes not only the wisdom of a

separation of powers, but also a dynamic of ethical considerations. It attempts to achieve a workable and functional
accommodation and unity of these considerations in a pluralistic society on the basis of several aspects of equality.

V
A Historical Perspective

Medieval Limitations on the Coercive Powers of Government

The predominant idea or orientation in the Middle Ages was not *equality* but *hierarchy*. The concept of the universe as a great hierarchical chain of being had its origin primarily in classical Greek philosophy (Lovejoy 1936, 24). The concept of hierarchy, however, can also be easily seen in Judeo-Christian religion and the military, economic, and social structure of feudal society, which was predominantly Germanic and pagan in origin. These were the major elements that went into the crucible of the Middle Ages in Europe which formed Western civilization. It is not such a paradox, therefore, that they are also the primary sources of our concepts of equality. In our colonial experience, religion was Christian, education was classical, and the legal system was English and based on feudal common law dating back to the Magna Charta.

As described in the brief historical preface, each of the three major ethical and legal systems that formed Western civilization at the time of the Middle Ages focused on a different aspect of human nature and perspective of the world in which we live. The ethical principles of universal equality are based on a universal moral duty of reverence and reciprocity in Judeo-Christian religion, on reason and reversibility in classical civilization, and on communal rights and responsibilities in the military, economic, and social relationships of Anglo-Saxon feudal structures. These also represent primarily deontological (based on duty), normative (based on norms or ideals), and communitarian (based on social tradition) ethical systems.

Both the natural law of classical civilization and Judeo-Christian monotheism had a concept of an order in the universe which placed the free will of human beings in a moral context. Throughout classical Greek literature, for example, there is a recognition that tyranny, excessive pride (hubris), and revenge lead to discord and tragedy. Correspondingly, throughout Judaic and Christian scripture there is the recognition that shalom (peace, wholeness, and harmony) depends not only on justice but also on atonement and forgiveness which lead to reconciliation. *Shalom, Islam,* and *salvation* all have either similar etymological roots (SLM) or meanings. The communitarian ethic of English society, originally based on custom and tradition, is somewhat unique in that it developed into a concept of rights for the free and equal individual with moral responsibility as the basis of communal solidarity. Custom and tradition are often given some of the validity of natural law concepts in so far as they represent the accumulated "right reason" of the community. These structured ethical systems developed into the legal structures of Roman Law, Canon Law, and common law which in the Middle Ages restricted the coercive powers of government.

This general framework in no way denies that the three major sources of Western civilization were certainly mixed ethical systems and also based, at least in the Middle Ages, on a concept of hierarchy. The concept of the moral authority of law deriving from the individual citizen would achieve prominence only later in the development of the modern state and constitutional democracy.

The Authority for Law Based on the Individual and Government by Consent

Our concept of the authority of law also being based on the morally responsible individual, government by consent, and the democratic process required a revolution in the hierarchical thought of the Middle Ages. Nevertheless, these concepts also had their origins in the democratic and republican traditions of Greece and Rome, in the Judeo-Christian concepts of covenant and compact, and in the Germanic traditions of election and contract. A revolution occurred in religion during the Reformation. A revolution in social, economic and cultural affairs occurred during the Renaissance. The scientific revolution changed the perceptions of both nature and cosmology and culminated in the Enlightenment. Each of these contributed to a revolution in thought which gave impetus to the notion of the individual, and his safety and happiness, being the basis of authority for government.

The Reformation challenged hierarchy within the church. Martin Luther developed the concepts of the priesthood of all believers and the stewardship of all callings or vocations to God. He also translated the Bible into German placing an emphasis on literacy. The Calvinist reformers developed democratic and representative forms of church government. Yet, the Presbyterian Samuel Rutherford in *Lex Rex* (1644) could argue for political equality under the Calvinist doctrine of original sin that all are equally depraved. A king, he wrote, "is under the same state of sin... of which he hath a share equally with all other men by nature... And if there be none a king by nature, there can be none a subject by nature" (Lakoff 1964, 61). The religious wars and persecutions forced the issue of religious pluralism within a political unity and eventually led to policies of toleration and freedom of conscience.

During the Renaissance, a philosophy of humanism developed the concept of the dignity and worth of the individual. The medieval unity based on hierarchy was also challenged by a revival of interest in classical civilization, a greater concern for individual education and development, a method of critical thought, secular concepts of the state, occasional republican forms of government, and a spirit of liberty. Greater social recognition was given to the arts and to the active life, to exploration and capitalism.

The other major influence challenging a tradition of hierarchy was the scientific revolution. The implications of the cosmology of Copernicus and its challenge to accepted authority are evident in the trial of Gallileo. René Descartes challenged the basis of all knowledge with his system of radical doubt, which lead to the subjective "I think, therefore I am." This was a search for certainty which also placed man back at the center of the universe, or at least at the center of a theory of knowledge. Perhaps more significant to the revolution in thought, however, was the development of empirical inductive thought and experimentation as a method to verify and compliment rational deductive thought and contemplation. A growing understanding of nature and the ability to use that knowledge lead to a greater concern with this world and secular matters. Knowledge, which had previously been understood as virtue, came to be understood as power.

James I, who was also the head of the Church of England, understood the political interconnection of these forms of revolutionary thought when he said "no bishop, no king" (Roberts, C. and Roberts, D. 1980, 328). The challenge to hierarchy as a mode of thought or paradigm was, indeed, best captured subsequently by a description of the more radical aspects of the Puritan Revolution as "the world turned upside down" (Hill 1975). In English feudal history, the Magna Charta was an aristocratic document, but it had egalitarian implications. By the time of the Puritan Revolution, Colonel Rainborough, a spokesman for the Levellers, would declare in the Putney debates:

> For really I think that the poorest he that is in England hath a life to live, as the greatest he; and therefore truly, sir, I think it clear, that every man that is to live

under a government ought first by his own consent
to put himself under that government; and I do think
that the poorest he in England is not at all bound in
the strict sense to that government that he hath not
had a voice to put himself under. (Lakoff 1964, 67)

A Transition in Constitutional Theory —
Coke and Locke

A major transitional figure in constitutional theory was Sir
Edward Coke. Coke was at the center of the struggle to prevent
the first Stuart king, James I, from using the royal prerogative
and the concept of the divine right of kings to interfere with the
constitutional law of England and traditional English rights
(Corwin, 1955; Roberts, C. and Roberts, D. 1980, chap. 13).
Coke represents a shift in the relationship between "higher
law" concepts of authority and the authority of procedural
democratic concepts of law.

In his *Second Institutes* and as a judge and eventually chief
justice of the King's Bench, Coke attempted to extend the
"common right and reason" of natural law and common law
to include procedural concepts of due process (Forkosch 1973).
In *Dr. Bonham's Case* (1610), for example, he stated that the
Royal College of Physicians, which had been incorporated by
Parliament, could not act as judges, ministers, and the recip-
ients of fines. In what was to become known as *Coke's Dictum*
he declared an Act of Parliament void:

One cannot be judge in his own case.... And it
appears in our books that in many cases the common law will control Acts of Parliament, and sometimes adjudge them to be utterly void. For when an
Act of Parliament is against common right and
reason, or repugnant, or impossible to be performed,

30

the common law will control it and adjudge such an
Act to be void.

In *Calvin's Case* (1608), he stated, "the law of nature cannot be
changed or taken away" and "should direct this case." Coke's
Dictum has been considered the single most important source
of what became in American constitutional law the concept of
judicial review.

In 1616, after pleading independence of the judiciary in
cases involving the king, Coke was dismissed from the bench.
He was subsequently, however, elected to Parliament in 1621.
There he used the Magna Charta as fundamental law to defend
the rights of Parliament, and Parliament as a court, to in turn
define and defend the fundamental law. As a member of
Parliament, Coke was a major force in developing the Petition
of Rights which declared unparliamentary taxation, billeting of
troops, arbitrary imprisonment, and martial law over civilians
all to be illegal. Coke was now using basically representative
procedural methods to validate concepts of due process and
traditional English rights.

Sir Edward Coke helped to define and defend the concept
of constitutional law, the concept of a fundamental law of the
land. There is a progression which extends from the Magna
Charta, the Petition of Rights, and the English Bill of Rights of
1689, to the Bill of Rights in the United States Constitution. Our
own constitutional process affirmed and politically validated
what were believed to be certain "higher law" principles.

A new synthesis and unity of thought developed in the later
part of the seventeenth century based on Isaac Newton's laws
of nature (Randall 1926, chap. XI). The concept was that of an
orderly mechanical universe, with the metaphor being that of
a clock and God as the clock maker. John Locke used such a
concept of nature and God to convert "higher law" concepts
into those of the natural rights of the free and equal individual
in a state of nature. Locke's natural rights include life, liberty,
and property and he intermingled these somewhat by stating
that one has a property in his own person. In the social contract

of Locke, limited powers are delegated to government because there is a need to define, adjudicate, and enforce laws
to protect both society and the safety of the individual. Government, however, is by consent.[7] Society has a right, therefore,
to overthrow a government that abuses its delegated powers.

Locke is a transitional figure because he helped change the
metaphor or paradigm by which we understand political
philosophy. His major political work was entitled *Two Treatises
on Government* (1690). In the first treatise he disassembled
patriarchy, the prevailing metaphor for hierarchy in both the
family and government. In his more famous second treatise,
Locke used the concept of a social contract between free and
equal individuals in a state of nature to translate theistic and
natural law concepts into the language of natural rights for the
individual. In the second treatise the individual is perceived to
not only have natural rights but also to be the source of authority for government.

The Integration of Ethical Traditions —
Kant, Jefferson, and Lincoln

William Barrett, in *The Death of the Soul,* considers
Immanuel Kant (1724-1804) to be "the last great thinker in
whom the intellectual unity of the Western mind is still held
together" (1986, 52). There are some parallels in his formu-
lations of the categorical imperative (the universal rule) to
metaphysical, natural law, communitarian and individual considerations. Treating human beings as an end and not as a
means, for example, could be considered to be a normative
ethic as well as a deontological ethic. Kant also, however,
subscribed to a new type of dualism in separating the knower
from that which is known. We cannot know a thing in itself, he
claimed, but only our perception of it. St. Augustine's theology
and philosophy had been self-reflective. Kant's theology and
philosophy, however, became self-referential. Kant's concept
of morality is based on universal equality but, because his

epistemology separates the knower from that which is known, it is not externally integrated. It is based on the rational individual as moral agent without concessions to God, nature, or a society of other moral agents.

I perceive a more satisfactory unity and integration of metaphysics, nature, social theory, and the nature of human beings in the eclectic moral thought of Thomas Jefferson. Jefferson's thought included Stoic, Christian, humanist, deist, and moral sense philosophy, but it also included Epicurean, utilitarian, agrarian, Enlightenment, social contract, and natural rights concepts (Koch 1943). God, nature, society, and individuals, however, were still all included in a pragmatic system that both understood a person to be a free and responsible moral agent and also was based on a concept of universal equality.

Both Kant and Jefferson had an intellectual span that was able to incorporate both the particular and the universal. Kant is perhaps seen as the culmination of the Enlightenment in that he was able to expand his self-referential reasoning from the particular to universal conclusions. Jefferson, on the other hand, often beginning with universals and self-evident truths, was able to relate them to the individual moral personality. Kant lived his entire life in the small town of Königsberg in East Prussia, yet he is credited with being among the first to postulate that there were other universes, other galaxies than our own. Jefferson, who is more correctly viewed as the beneficiary of a diverse humanist tradition, was a prime example of what we think of as a Renaissance man — broad, diverse, and international in his thought and actions. Yet, in an addendum to his autobiography, he wrote that he thought that the most important contribution a person could make was to introduce a new plant to his native soil (Koch 1943, 190; Padover 1943, 1288).

Kant, in his own thought, separated theology from empirical knowledge. Jefferson, on the other hand, was instrumental in separating religion from the coercive power of government. Jefferson understood that one of his most important works was the Statute of Virginia for Religious Freedom.

Though one can easily find fault with Jefferson and some of his writings, it is very important to understand that for him the self-evident truth that "all men are created equal" was a universal moral assertion. Jefferson felt that nature was the work of a God who was "Nature's God," the Architect, the Creator, the First Cause. Human beings were in this sense created equal. They are also equal he felt in that they are "endowed by their Creator with certain unalienable rights" which include "life, liberty, and the pursuit of happiness." Indeed, it was to secure these rights associated with the moral assertion of universal equality that "Governments are instituted amongst men, deriving their just powers from the consent of the governed." The Declaration of Independence is argued in the manner of Euclidean geometry. It is also significant to note in this context that, unlike Locke, Jefferson did not include property in his first principles or axioms.

More specifically, Jefferson felt that we all share equally a common humanity in that we have a capacity for, and possess, a moral sense (Padover 1943, 1032-34). In a letter to his young friend Peter Carr, Jefferson wrote:

He who made us would have been a pitiful bungler, if he had made the rules of our conduct a matter of science. For one man of science, there are a thousand who are not. What would have become of them? Man was destined for society. His morality, therefore, was to be formed to this object. He was endowed with a sense of right and wrong merely relative to this. This sense is as much a part of his nature, as the sense of hearing, seeing, feeling; it is the true foundation of morality.... The moral sense, or conscience, is as much a part of man as his leg or his arm. It is given to all human beings in a stronger or weaker degree.... It may be strengthened by exercise, as may any particular limb of the body. This sense is submitted, indeed in some degree, to the guidance of reason; but it is a small stock which is required for this; even a less one than what we call Common sense. State a moral case to a ploughman and a professor. The former will decide it as well, and often better than the latter, because he has not been led astray by artificial rules. (Peterson 1977, 424)

Jefferson's respect for the moral agency of others was indeed an affirmation of his own humanity, a self-affirmation. Concerning women he wrote, "It is civilization alone which replaces women in the enjoyment of their natural equity. That first teaches us to subdue the selfish passions, and to respect those rights in others that we respect in ourselves" (Jefferson [1785] 1972, 60). Jefferson was opposed to religious, political, and social tyranny; thus, equality for him was also a matter of self-assertion. His method of dealing with the will to power of human beings was to invert it to a will to resist the despotism or tyranny of others. In a letter to the physician Benjamin Rush he wrote, "I have sworn upon the altar of God, eternal hostility against every form of tyranny over the mind of men" (Bartlett 1968, 472).

A universal moral sense or conscience was for Jefferson a basis of our common humanity and natural equality. It was what made persons capable of determining their own form of government by consent. This equality was for Jefferson universal and it included women, American Indians (Jefferson [1785] 1972, 227), and blacks (Jefferson [1785] 1972, 142). It was a matter of both self-affirmation and self-assertion, and this can help us understand his great concern for religious freedom, public education, and the injustice of slavery.

Slavery was the tragic flaw in the founding of American government. Jefferson was a slaveholder and this cannot be dismissed as only a concession to the society in which he lived. It was in his own self-interest and it allowed him to live an aristocratic lifestyle. He thus contributed to this tragedy. Yet, he understood the moral bankruptcy of slavery, its moral incompatibility with democratic government, and the need for its eventual abolition.

Jefferson felt that slavery could not be immediately abolished without the threat of great violence because of past injustices to blacks and the deeply held prejudices of whites. He had unsuccessfully recommended laws which would have achieved gradual but total emancipation, colonization of gradually emancipated slaves, and exclusion of slavery from all Western Territories (see also Jefferson [1785] 1972, 214). His diatribe against the king for allowing slavery to become established in the colonies was omitted from the final draft of the Declaration of Independence. At the time of the Missouri Compromise of 1820, he described the threat of the slavery issue to the Union as a "firebell in the night," and he wrote, "we have a wolf by the ears, and we can neither hold him, nor safely let him go. Justice is in the one scale, and self-preservation in the other" (Peterson 1977, 568). More than thirty years earlier he had written, "I tremble for my country when I reflect that God is just; that his justice cannot sleep forever..." (Jefferson [1785] 1972, 163).

Jefferson's proposal to abolish slavery after 1800 in all territories and future territories was defeated in committee by one vote. Concerning this he later commented: "Thus we see the fate of millions of unborn hanging on the tongue of one man, and heaven was silent in that awful moment" (Kenyon 1980). Jefferson understood the moral dimensions of freedom and he put them forth in stating the ideals of a new nation.

In practice, a civil war and several constitutional amendments were necessary to make universal equality as a principle and as the basis of the democratic process something of a reality. The issue over which there finally could be no compromise on slavery was the political assertion by John C. Calhoun and some in the southern states that slavery was not a moral wrong that had to be tolerated temporarily, but that it was a positive good.

Lincoln never wavered in his assertion that slavery was morally wrong and he opposed its extension into the territories. He also opposed resolving the issue of slavery in the territories, as Senator Douglas had proposed, by making it a matter of local popular sovereignty. Yet, he initially fought, and probably could not have otherwise won, the Civil War on the issue of popular sovereignty and majority rule in a democratic republic. To preserve the Union, Lincoln needed both public opinion and the slaveholding border states of Missouri, Kentucky, Maryland, and Delaware.

Lincoln tried to uphold both the ideal in the Declaration of Independence of "a new nation, conceived in Liberty, and dedicated to the proposition that all men are created equal" and the rule of law in the Constitution of "government of the people, by the people, for the people."[8] Lincoln realized, however, that public opinion was needed to bring the ideals of universal equality into practice in a democratic republic.

VI
Conclusions, Current Reflections, and Summary

Conclusions

A secure future for our system of government does not require a different set of moral principles from those in the Declaration of Independence and our Constitution. Even great reformers, such as Martin Luther King, have simply asked that we put our original principles into practice. It is our difficulty in fully living up to our own ideals, individually and collectively, that has been referred to as the "promise of disharmony" (Huntington 1981). The future of constitutional democracy depends upon our continued efforts to reconcile our ideals and principles with the democratic process.

What was unique about James Madison and the Founding Fathers, however, was not just that they based government on the consent of the people, but that they based government on individuals and a people that they understood to be not always virtuous. The limitations and divisions, the checking of interest by interest, and the placing of constitutional law above the divisions of government were all directed toward placing restraints on both factions and majorities. Yet it was understood that in a pluralistic society the alternative to government by deliberation based on equality was government based on simple coercion or privilege. For this reason Madison understood the importance of the republican experiment that Jefferson called "the world's best hope" (Padover 1943, 385) and Lincoln called "the last, best hope of earth" (Basler 1953, vol. V, 537).

The United States Constitution was originally concerned primarily with freedoms from the potential abuses of governmental power. Since the Civil War, the dynamic political system created by that constitution, however, has responded to political change and public opinion to address enabling freedoms and other moral issues of equality. The political franchise has been expanded almost universally. Other issues have been the definition of legal equality, an equality of opportunity and education, and more recently some issues of social equality. The degree of economic inequality has also been in part addressed with such measures as the curtailing of the excesses of laissez faire capitalism, a progressive income tax, and the development of a social welfare state.

Reflective writers, such as George Orwell, have urged us to accept the political, economic, and moral responsibilities of freedom because they were aware of how easily freedom can be lost. That is, if we value freedom, then we should establish the conditions for freedom and its survival. The several aspects of universal equality do provide a moral context for freedom and pluralism. It is the moral assertion of the dignity and worth of each individual, and its translation into several aspects of political equality concerning the coercive powers of government, that makes the accommodation and preservation of a wide variety of attributes, abilities, and desires possible.

Alexis de Tocqueville understood correctly, however, that equality misunderstood can threaten freedom. Indeed, equality misunderstood can threaten virtue or any moral distinction. Neither unrestricted equality nor unrestricted freedom can, therefore, serve as the practical basis of a pluralistic political community. American constitutional democracy is an attempt to reconcile and integrate these several ideals and principles — not only the sometimes conflicting claims of freedom and equality, but also the several different aspects of equality based on the multi-faceted nature of human beings. Such an understanding of our governmental system leaves us with an indeterminate but dynamic politics.[9]

Concerning *values*, ethics does involve the making of distinctions concerning right and wrong, perceived truth and justice, the common good, and distinctions in individual character and virtue. Whenever a hierarchy of *persons* is used to justify coercive power, however, it is often coercive power that ends up sustaining the hierarchy. The colonial founders were concerned with such abuse of the coercive powers of government by self-appointed and hereditary elites of kings, priests, and nobles. Jefferson could hardly be described as a Hobbesian or a Calvinist but he wrote, "Mankind soon learn to make interested uses of every right and power which they possess, or may assume" (Jefferson [1785] 1972, 121). He also wrote that he knew of "no safe depository of the ultimate powers of society but the people themselves..." (Malone, vol. 6, 353). Lincoln said simply, "No man is good enough to govern another man without that other's consent" (Basler 1953, vol. II, 226).

United States constitutional democracy attempts to achieve accommodation and resolution of conflict in a pluralistic society, without arbitrary coercion or alienation. It attempts to do this by limiting and dividing the powers of government and recognizing several aspects of equality. It is also a means, however, of collectively achieving and securing a wide spectrum of goals and values. Self-government or the development and expression of the mature, responsible personality, in the context of community, can itself, for example, be considered a moral goal.

After devoting much of his life to a study of the history of freedom, Lord Acton, an eighteenth century English historian, concluded that "Power tends to corrupt and absolute power corrupts absolutely" (Bartlett 1968, 750). A corollary might be added to this concerning sovereignty and the coercive powers of government — a system of political equality rewards virtue and merit more readily than a personal political hierarchy recognizes moral issues of equality. The constitutional democracy of the United States protects individual differences in beliefs and opinions. Within limits the government both allows and makes distinctions concerning values, natural circumstances, social conditions, and behavior. Although we must acknowledge our shortcomings in history, it is very important to recognize and understand that United States constitutional democracy also affirms an *equality of persons*. That is its primary moral assertion.

Current Reflections

The international political tragedy of the twentieth century, a century which coined the word genocide, bears witness to the need for universal concepts of equality. The basic political problem remains a tendency to divide the world and society into "we" versus "they", the inability to morally recognize our common humanity. The alienation of our times would also tend to affirm the need for integration — the need to individually and politically integrate the composite nature of our own humanity as well as the several aspects of the world in which we live.[10] Singular theories that have based order and moral authority on *only* material needs, an aspect of social conscience, reason, or a metaphysical or religious concept, or *only* on the individual, the state, natural science, or ideology, have often led to disintegration and individual or communal tragedy. By focusing on even perhaps a particular truth, in a quest for certainty, they have too easily justified the use of coercive force or been the cause of alienation.

Nor is it easy to imagine a resolution of the problems of alienation in our own society if individual rights and freedoms are not also understood in a moral context and associated with responsibilities. Individual rights and freedoms need to be understood in the larger ethical contexts of moral duty and reciprocity, normative behavior and reversibility, communal values and responsibilities, and a commitment to defend similar rights and freedoms for others.

Furthermore, it is difficult to imagine an adequate resolution of the global problems which have resulted from technology without a concept of universal equality and our common humanity. Several writers, perhaps the most prominent being Konrad Lorenz, have noted that our technical progress has far exceeded the parameters of our biological adaptive mechanisms and moral structures. Among the problems which threaten the future of all peoples are those of nuclear or biological warfare, genetic engineering and population control in a time of scarce resources and a threatened environment, and the level of totalitarianism and terrorism which technology has made possible.

Even from the view of evolutionary development, it can be argued that natural selection may not favor a species that is unable to control aggression with structured ethical systems. A more balanced evolutionary theory, a greater understanding of the nearly symbiotic nature of our own biology, and game theory have all recently emphasized the importance of cooperation as a factor of natural selection (Axelrod 1984; Thomas 1975; Dawkins 1989, chap. 12). Ethical structure and cooperation are significant elements in the fitness of natural selection, much as they are often factors for peace and tranquility in psychology, sociology, natural law theory, and religion.

Summary

An analytical framework for moral and political philosophy has been presented. This framework takes into account the composite and integral nature of human beings and the several ways that we relate to the world in which we live. It is only meant to be a scaffolding and, therefore, it is far from complete. It does, however, provide a basis for understanding the several different aspects of universal equality which provide the moral foundations of United States constitutional democracy. These different aspects of universal equality are also derived historically in Western civilization from ethical and legal systems which are a prescriptive or instructional type of knowledge and faith. The government of the United States is a constitutional democracy. Only be referring to it as such, can we understand the several aspects of its "central idea" of universal equality. In our system of government, universal equality is a "higher law" substantive principle concerning the dignity and worth of all persons and it is also the basis of a procedural concept of equality in the democratic process. The moral aspects of universal equality exclude the coercive powers of government from certain parts of our lives and give accountability to the divisions of government which make, adjudicate, and enforce our laws. We certainly need to recognize the value of other cultures, of other metaphors for understanding the nature of human beings and how we relate to the world in which we live, and of other frameworks of analysis. It is within the several aspects of universal equality, however, that all people can both assert their individuality against tyranny and also affirm their humanity.

By balancing the several aspects of universal equality, constitutional democracy in the United States achieves some recognition and integration of the individual, social, and natural moral constraints within which we live. Our form of government, however, is also a recognition that some of our highest aspirations, strongest commitments, and deepest faiths neither can nor should be coerced by government.

Notes

1. See "Memory and Truth" by Craig Dykstra (1987) for a discussion of the role of memory in these functions.

2. It is understood that these categories are very general and that a capacity such as social conscience relates to several sometimes conflicting ethical concerns of "society" such as family, community, nationality, and inclusive humanity.

3. Regarding our need to orientate ourselves in both space and time, see Mircea Eliade's works *The Sacred and the Profane* (1961) and *The Myth of the Eternal Return* (1974).

4. Madison hoped that the Bill of Rights "might acquire by degree the character of fundamental maxims of free government, and as they become incorporated into the national sentiment, counteract the impulses of interest and passion" (see Diamond 1979, 71).

5. Jefferson appreciated and attempted to emphasize the difference between constitutional and legislative processes (Jefferson [1785] 1972, 120-129).

6. "The *Nicomachean Ethics* exhibits indecision between two accounts of *eudaimonia* — a comprehensive and an intellectualist account. According to the intellectualist account, stated in Book X Chap. 7, *eudaimonia* is realized in the activity of the most divine part of man, functioning in accordance with its proper excellence. This is the activity of theoretical contemplation. According to the comprehensive account (described

as secondary at 1178a 9) *eudaimonia* essentially involves not just the activity of the theoretical intellect, but the full range of human life and action, in accordance with the broader excellences of moral virtue and practical wisdom. This view connects *eudaimonia* with the conception of human nature as composite, i.e. as involving the interaction of reason, emotion, perception, and action in an ensouled body" (Nagel 1972, 252).

7. The transition in theory is from citizenship by birthright to citizenship by consent (see Schuck and Smith 1985, chap. 1). Each concept of citizenship by itself has inherent problems.

8. It is probably not just a coincidence that these quotes are from the first and last lines of the Gettysburg Address.

9. "In large measure, a political judgment is usually 'judicial' in quality; that is, for the most part it involves a judgment concerning conflicting claims, all of which possess a certain validity. As Aristotle shrewdly pointed out, there is no problem of political judgment when one claim alone is admitted to be valid and enthroned above all the rest. The result of this condition, however, is that the political association is replaced by a state of siege (*Politics,* III, xiii, 1283a 21-1283b). But once the political association is defined as a compound of many diverse parts, and once it is allowed that these 'parts' will have different opinions, interests, and claims, the politicalness of the judgment will depend on a sensitivity to diversities. A political judgment, in other words, is 'true' when it is public, not public when it accords to some standard external to politics" (Wolin 1960, 63).

10. Shirley Letwin describes integration as part of the cultural characteristics of the gentleman in *The Gentlemen in Trollope: Individuality and Moral Conduct* (1983). Kenneth Minogue did an excellent review of this book (1983).

References

Axelrod, Robert. 1984. *The Evolution of Cooperation*. New York: Basic Books.

Barrett, William. 1986. *Death of the Soul*. Garden City, N.Y.: Anchor Press/Doubleday.

Bartlett, John. 1968. *Familiar Quotations*, fourteenth edition. Boston: Little, Brown.

Basler, Roy P., ed., 1953. *The Collected Works of Abraham Lincoln*, 8 vols. New Brunswick, N.J.: Rutgers University.

Calvin's Case. 1608. 7 Co. Rep. 15b.

Corwin, Edward S. 1955. *The "Higher Law" Background of American Constitutional Law*. Ithica, N.Y.: Cornell University.

Davis, David Brion. 1990. *Revolutions: Reflections on American Equality and Foreign Liberations*. Cambridge, Mass.: Harvard University.

Dawkins, Richard. 1989. *The Selfish Gene*. New York: Oxford University.

Diamond, Martin. 1979. "Ethics and Politics: The American Way." In *The Moral Foundations of the American Republic*, ed. Robert H. Horwitz. Charlottesville, Va.: University of Virginia.

Dr. Bonham's Case. 1610. 8 Co. 118a.

Dykstra, Craig. 1987. "Memory and Truth." *Theology Today*, vol. XLIV, No. 2.

Eliade, Mircea. 1961. *The Sacred and the Profane*. New York: Harper and Brothers.

Eliade, Mircea. 1974. *The Myth of the Eternal Return*. Princeton, N.J.: Princeton University.

Foner, Phillip, ed., 1950. *Basic Writings of Thomas Jefferson*. Garden City, N.Y.: Halcyon House.

Forkosch, Morris D. 1973. "Due Process in Law." In *Dictionary of the History of Ideas*, ed. Phillip P. Wiener. New York: Charles Scribner's Sons.

Hamilton, Alexander, James Madison, and John Jay. [1787-88] 1961. *The Federalist Papers*. New York: New American Library.

Hill, Christopher. 1975. *The World Turned Upside Down*. Harmondsworth, Middlesex, England: Penguin Books.

Hobbes, Thomas [1651] 1981. *Leviathon*, ed. C. B. Macpherson. Harmondsworth, Middlesex, England: Penguin Books.

Huntington, Samuel P. 1981. *American Politics: The Promise of Disharmony*. Cambridge, Mass.: Harvard University.

Jaffa, Henry V. 1982 ed. *Crisis of the House Divided: An Interpretation of the Issues of the Lincoln-Douglas Debates*. Chicago: University of Chicago.

Jefferson, Thomas [1785] 1972. *Notes on the State of Virginia*. New York: W.W. Norton and Company.

Kenyon, Cecelia M. 1980. "Thomas Jefferson." In the *Encyclopaedia Britannica*, 15th Edition, 30 vol. Chicago: Encyclopaedia Britannica.

Koch, Adrienne. 1943. *The Philosophy of Thomas Jefferson*. New York: Columbia University.

Kohlberg, Lawrence. 1981. *The Philosophy of Moral Development*, vol. I. San Francisco: Harper and Row.

Konner, Melvin. 1983. *The Tangled Wing: Biological Constraints on the Human Spirit*. New York: Harper Colophon.

Lakoff, Sanford A. 1964. *Equality in Political Philosophy.* Cambridge, Mass.: Harvard University.

Letwin, Shirley Robin. 1982. *The Gentleman in Trollope: Individuality and Moral Conduct.* Cambridge, Mass.: Harvard University.

Lovejoy, Arthur O. 1936. *The Great Chain of Being.* Cambridge, Mass.: Harvard University.

Malone, Dumas. 1981. *Jefferson and His Time,* 6 vol. Boston: Little, Brown.

Marbury v. Madison. 1803. 1 cranch 137.

McWilliams, Wilson Carey. 1979. "On Equality as the Moral Foundation for Community." In *The Moral Foundations of The American Republic,* ed. Robert H. Horwitz. Charlottesville, Va.: University of Virginia.

Meyers, Marvin, ed., 1981. *The Mind of the Founder; Sources of the Political Thought of James Madison,* revised ed. Hanover, N.H.: Brandeis University.

Minogue, Kenneth. 1983. "The Culture of the Gentleman." *Public Interest* No. 71, Spring.

Nagel, Thomas. 1972. "Aristotle on Eudaimonia." *Phronesis* 17:252-59.

Padover, Saul K., ed., 1943. *The Complete Jefferson.* New York: Tudor Publishing.

Paine, Thomas. [1776] 1982. Common Sense, ed. Isaac Kramnick. Harmondsworth, Middlesex, England: Penguin Books.

Peterson, Merrill D., ed., 1977. *The Portable Thomas Jefferson.* New York: Penguin Books.

Pollack, Ervin H. 1979. *Jurisprudence: Principles and Applications.* Columbus, Oh.: Ohio State University.

Randall, John Herman. 1926. *The Making of the Modern Mind.* New York: Columbia University.

Rawls, John. 1971. *A Theory of Justice*. Cambridge, Mass.: Harvard University.

Roberts, Clayton, and David Roberts. 1980. *A History of England*, 2 vol. Englewood Cliffs, N.J.: Prentice-Hall.

Sabine, George H., and Thomas L. Thorson. 1973. *A History of Political Theory*, 4th ed. Hinsdale, Ill.: Dryden Press.

Sagan, Carl. 1978. *The Dragons of Eden: Speculations on the Evolutions of Human Intelligence*. New York: Ballantine Books.

Schuck, Peter H., and Rogers M. Smith. 1985. *Citizenship without Consent: Illegal Aliens in the American Polity*. New Haven: Yale University.

Stevenson, Leslie. 1987. *Seven Theories of Human Nature*. New York: Oxford University.

Thomas, Lewis. 1975. *The Lives of a Cell*. New York: Bantam Books.

Weber, Max. [1921] 1964. *The Theory of Economic and Social Organization*, 1st Paperback edition, ed. Talcott Parsons. New York: Free Press.

Wills, Garry. 1979. *Inventing America: Jefferson's Declaration of Independence*. New York: Vintage Books.

Wolin, Sheldon S. 1960. *Politics and Vision*. Boston: Little, Brown.